Ballads of Lost Lenoria

A Shadow's Cry Anthology

By Anthony Uyl

Devoted Publishing

Ingersoll, Ontario, Canada 2019

Ballads of Lost Lenoria

A Shadow's Cry Anthology

By Anthony Uyl

Contact us at: devotedpub@hotmail.com
Visit us on Facebook: @DevotedPublishing
See the full catalogue of Devoted Publishing books at:
http://www.lulu.com/spotlight/devotedpublishing

Published in Ingersoll, Ontario, Canada 2019

ISBN: 978-1-77356-388-6

Table of Contents

Introduction

So, this is a short collection of epic fantasy poetry. Given for mainly a table-top gaming audience but easily enjoyable by anyone. My passion for fantasy has been with me since I first read the greatest of fantasy epics in elementary and high school. There are elements of inspiration from all sorts of fantasy tropes, some will be easily recognizable, others you may need to do an internet search for to figure them out. And of course, there are biblical references as my faith would lead me to include these kinds of ideas in them.

I hope you enjoy this small volume. May it be the first of many to come!

- Anthony Uyl, President/Owner Devoted Publishing, Authour

Lost Lenoria

A time long ago, forgotten to ages,
When rivers ran clear and blue,
The sea was treacherous,
The storms glorious and angry.
Yahweh spoke a world into being,
Formed from his will alone,
He created something pure and good,
Along with the hosts of heaven.
Spirits of ages past knelt to the lord of heaven,
But some rebelled and ruined this new world,
This new Lenoria, into corruption and despair.
They led races of men, elves and dwarves,
To war against the gates of heaven.
Dragons raged the countryside,
Ancient demons burned the hearts of men,
Yet the ones that called on Yahweh's name,
Marched on the gates of Gehennorg,
To overthrow the rebellious king.
Blood was spilt, oaths were sworn,
Bound to an ancient gem, lost to time,
Was the lord of the demon host.
Though he raged against time,
For ages he has ruled,
Now bound to world he despised.
Peace reigned for a while,
But for how long?
Eventually the hearts of mortals gave way,
Evil found its root once more,
It is time for the righteous to stand firm,
To reclaim Lenoria once more.

The Elf Maid

And as the elven princess trod,
Along a road she had long forgot,
She dreamed of him, the forgotten king,
Of who her dreams and songs did sing.

Her father bid her go aloft,
To lands long gone, away and soft,
Yet hard she chose the life to live,
Her very life to darkness give.

To face the shadow that has grown,
In the east that where haunts are known,
She'd rather face the growing night,
Even if it ever be her fright.

The king of man did forget her not,
Bearing her jewel with loyal fraught,
He dreamed of her but did not hope,
That united they'd be to forever cope.

She sent him love that he could not bear,
For he wished her to leave to realms so fair,
To be with her people to forget him so,
But her thoughts ever drifted to him not to go.

Though wars were fought and legions lost,
She did care not about that cost,
Though blood was shed upon the cusp,
She knew he'd come just as he must.

For love so strong did she uphold,
Even if he convinced himself not told,
Yet she believed forever true,
That her elven blood ran right and blue.

The lady of light knew her heart,
That she could never him depart,
There was purity in her golden mind,
That no man will every truly find.

Though the fires of darkness spread,
She'll find her heart though when dead,
The flames of war do drain her heart,
That the man of life shall 'ere depart.

While hope may seem to all be lost,
There is no doubt to her the cost,
Though she doth die in pain of loss,
She dare not give in to the dirge and dross.

Where there be hope she doth believe,
That truth will ever come to conceive,
That he will return to her warm arms,
And sing to him her dearest songs.

Dark Rider Hunting

Hunting, searching, ever onwards,
For his masters forgotten glory,
The dark rider terrifying to behold,
Runs down the enemy to the fire.

An enemy anew threatens the land,
With determination to destroy,
The glory of the dark one,
A master that shall rule the land.

The dark rider gallops, upon a steed.
Given to them by someone they will betray,
But they know it not,
They pay their tribute to them, loyally.

But the glory of the fire, needs to be sated,
There it is traversing the land,
Once they were defeated by a king,
But not again, they will find the bearer, the great enemy.

Destruction is their name,
Ghosts of a forgotten age,
They rose at their masters' call,
Now they hunt forever for his beloved.

Only time will allow them to find,
The treacherous one of the new enemy,
That will inevitably be enslaved,
For his rebellion against their lord.

Gallop, dark rider,
Time is growing short,
The glory marches ever towards doom,
Time is short, the light is about to shine.

Dwarf King

Stalwart fighter, with a devoted heart,
The dwarf wields his axe so smart,
To cleave the orc and goblin alike,
Fighting ever onward, sharp as spikes.

The mountain hold cannot contain the grudge,
Towards the ones that betrayed the trudge,
When the fled their home from the fires wrath,
Only to return to halls torn from craft.

The warrior sits on a stone throne,
In the place once again his home,
After felling the invading tide,
To which he never tried to hide.

His brothers and kin hold his ear,
To give him tidings of things to bear,
The days are dark, evil has come,
It is not like them to go and run from.

The dwarven fighter cleaves to his will,
Just like gold that haunts him still,
To take vengeance on the realm of wood,
That hosts the evil that ever it could.

Spiders of old, and goblins of hate
Have tried to cower from him, but too late,
There is fire in his soul to reclaim the throes,
Of all that has been taken from him in rows.

Awaiting the Dawn

Wayward wanderer, traveling roads,
Forgotten and forlorn, in quiet country-sides,
Watching for evil tides, to sweep from the east,
Where the shadow grows, ever constant.

Creatures of darkness aroused by fright,
Broken by ancient vows sworn long ago,
To a dark lord that cares for nothing,
Nothing but himself and his will.

The wanderer travels on, watching the shadow,
Fighting the tide of grief that rolls ever on,
To make for hope that yet may die,
As long as he and his own do not fail in their duty.

Flowers of beauty that he fights for,
The dawning sun, ever warm,
To defend the wonderful world of old,
To await the dawn, and the joy it brings.

Hunt Some Orc

Run through the trees,
Evergreen and fragrant,
To chase the aberration,
The abomination,
That ruins the land,
Despoils the beauty of spring.
Avoiding the sunlight,
To bring the monster to bear,
Freeing captives,
Caught for food,
Blood pumps in our veins.
We must hurry,
The little ones won't last.
Heroes we are,
Set out to preserve,
The innocence of children,
By hunting some orc!

The Elven Queen

Fair and radiant,
The grass shines in her presence,
Gowns of pure daylight,
Draw around her.
To make her beauty emanate,
Hair of twilight,
Calls on the coming dawn,
That the sun will shine the fairer.
Light itself calls her name,
She commands the moon,
To rise in the night,
The sun to come at the time.
Sands of time can't hold her,
As she gleams in pure star light.
Immortal, beautiful,
Even dwarves pay her dues,
For nothing shall ever be called fairer,
Then the Elven Queen.

The Necromancer

Black robes filling the night
Breath of noxious vapors
Insects flee at the sight
Wolves come to the beckoned call.
Lords of death dance in the night
The dark one stands in solace
There is little life to be found
Where the lifeless one dawns.
He stretches out his hand
That eldritch energy may flow
Daylight crumbles at the call
As the ground begins to move.
A bone champion emerges
Free from the ever decay
Knowledge lost in twilight doom
To serve is to live.
A smile creeps forth
The warrior has come
What blasphemy will he taunt
As the necromancer calls his legion.

The Red Dragon

Iron scales concealing a cruel soul
Devouring innocent creatures.
He sits on a mountain of glittering
Gold.
Magic infuses the bones of the ancient wyrm
Damnation is his eternal calling.
Though nature be not his nurture
He gives in to the anger within
Of a mad world that pales his own
Sin.
The blasphemous name given him
By a wizard of long past due
There belongs no salvation to him.
Towns are razed and heroes consumed
All to his sadistic glee.
What divine and arcane power
Can liberate the world from his rage
Only the true power of Yeshua
Can bring him to his knees.
Until judgement comes there is little
Anyone can hope to attain
To fulfill his dark delights.
Where oh Lamb is your power?
The Lion that will curb his strength?
You will be subdued wyrm,
In slow and precious time!

Mountain Caretakers

Delving deep in mountains,
Gold that covets the hearts of men,
The dwarves rule with absolution,
Knowing that ever they will reign.
All desire the mountain,
Elves, humans, halflings,
Even the ancient dragons of old,
Yet none shall take these halls of stone,
From masters so wise and strong,
That the fortress is impregnable.
Many have tried, all have failed,
The fields of Achaiaer are stained in blood,
The blood of mortals and immortals alike,
The gods themselves may be powerless,
To strip the hall from the mountain king.
Ever was there mountains so tall,
A ridge of peaks that lined,
The spine of a world long forgotten,
Orcs used to rule here,
Now they are banished,
Relegated to realms of other weaker mortals.
They rule with surety,
Thinking they cannot be uprooted,
Yet evil arises,
Unlike anything seen before,
The king of lies has arisen,
A dark prince to come,
And demand his due,
Or watch these dwarves burn,
Burn in the inferno of eternity.

Giant Tyrants

A race of old,
Beyond the written word,
They arose from illicit marriages,
Born from the seed of angels and man.
The gods forbid it,
Yahweh himself condemned it,
Sending storms to punish the arrival,
Yet they survive.
Some walk dead,
Other rule in palaces of gold and crystal,
Yet their fury is still felt,
Enslaving nations to pay heed,
To a dark lord in the north,
That uses power of an unnatural sort.
Magic some call it,
Miracles others refer it,
Not right for mortal creatures is for certain,
Corrupting hearts and minds.
The lord of the fires,
Scourging the land and skies,
Comes for his own,
These kings and tyrants to form his kingdom,
And an army that will not be stopped.
Hundreds of thousands line their ranks,
Slaves and freemen alike march in black armour,
To enslave the world.
Who will rise to save the feeble,
And bring the age of peace,
Promised so long ago?

An Adventure

I sit here, peacefully,
No cares, no wonders, no desires,
Then I see you walk past,
Eyes so wonderous and I think,
What roads shall I travel?
What mountains shall I climb?
What forest shall I wander?
What rivers shall I swim?
To find the truest treasure,
Any man or elf could find,
To be enraptured by a maiden,
So elven, so divine.
I have no desire for gold,
Or treasures so bold and bright,
I once desired quiet,
The peace from the cool evening,
I promised myself I wound not,
Go out into the danger alone,
But there was something calling me,
That I had to leave my very home.
Break open my heart,
See what it is I would find,
To bring peace to my homeland,
Where no shadow will divide.
You bid me not go,
But it is evident to me,
That if I do not leave now,
I will never be at peace.

Forest for the Trees

The old world is passing away,
While the machine of industry comes,
Hopefully the old ways will not die,
As the wisdom it truly holds.
While the trees fall and ashen,
The elven lords do weep,
Their home is slowly fading,
And dreams fall ever so deep.
Though they war and string their bows,
The orc army marches onward,
To claim the precious forests,
For their dark lord in the north.
The slender and grace of the trees,
No other land can attest to,
Its majesty is unparalleled,
Nothing can compare to it.
Wisdom is held in those branches,
Wisdom of ages long gone,
If trees could speak, they would tell you,
Of when old races long gone, walked about.
The memories of old are slowly passing away,
As the dark forces hack and burn,
To make way for something new,
Something unwanted in this world.
Stand and fight for the forest's wisdom,
Elves march to war,
The queen of the trees will call you all,
To defend its beauty once more.

Evil Wizard

Scheming to rule men,
Not holding to his lofty place,
A tower built for evil,
While an army grows below him.
He writes his spells to conquer,
All the realms below him,
A servant of darker evils,
Though he does not know it.
The demons that speak to him in silence,
Tell him secrets long forgotten,
The lord of fire wants to devour him,
To take his power for his own.
The evil wizard plots destruction,
To grow power and greed,
He cares not at all for living things,
Just the necromantic arts, long lost.
Recruiting armies through treachery,
He walks about unseen,
Learning the secrets of mortal hearts,
So that he can offer lies unclean.
People fall to his sway,
His words sound true and just,
Yet filled with lies and malice,
There is nothing he will not promise.
He will not deliver on his word,
He means nothing true or pure,
By the time the slaves realize it,
They are already tainted beyond redemption.
Time to stand and fight for justice,
To rip his tower down,
Can the forces of light conjure,
Someone to ride to war and freedom?

Fortress of Heaven

Hewn of solid rock,
Standing tall over the rivers of old,
A fortress of men stands,
Stands to protect the mortal realms.
Wars have raged against this place,
To take down and feed of human blood,
But the craftsmanship of dwarves,
The cunning of elves,
Has never broken its gates down.
Many have tried,
Orcs, goblins, dark elves, hobgoblins,
All have tried to claim this place as their own.
None have succeeded,
Though the skill of men in battle,
Is limited compared to the ancient,
To the warlike races,
They have always held true to the protection,
The sturdiness of walls built long ago.
Graceful, yet strong.
Elegant, yet thick.
This fortress is a testament to things,
Of ancient alliances from millennia ago.
Many have tried to claim ownership over it,
Those that have long ago abandoned it,
For its halls and rooms are many and strong,
But the race of humanity has held it ever true.
They guard it as a royal sanctum,
Given to them by the gods themselves.
The darkness is coming though,
They must prepare,
For the gates of the Fortress of Heaven,
May not hold back this new, yet ancient, evil.

Orc Lord

Where he comes from, no one knows,
He has fought in wars uncounted,
Bled more mortals than can be numbered,
All fear his name when it passes their tongues.
Baladan, the black orc of Beelzebub,
First of his master's servants.
He fights for not reason,
Other than to feast on human flesh,
Once, he too, was a human,
But his dark master made him corrupt,
And perfect for evil.
Although time should have claimed his soul,
Immortal he has become,
Many have thought to have slain him dead,
Yet time and time again,
He rides new hordes to war.
Never will he find peace,
Until the world is covered in flame,
At his master's command.
He desires nothing than to carve new flesh,
To break the souls of all,
To make them bow before him,
And be enslaved to the will of the dark father.
He cares not for gold, or jewels,
Just blood of flesh.
For conquering.
The storm is coming when orcs will come,
With Baladan at their head,
Heroes will need to rise up,
If he is to be taken down,
For the world to have hope once more.

Elven Lord

Regal, majestic,
He rides on a white horse,
Bred for war,
To free the mortal realms from despair.
His blades dance in battle,
While the enemy cannot approach,
Without feeling the touch of steel,
The cold release of life.
Many years of training,
Have given him glorious skill,
Even in arts of kingship,
To rule with justice and might.
None question his wisdom,
He has tried the greatest and best,
His learning is beyond compare,
Even the ancient wizards do not equal.
When the world comes to the brink of war,
He will respond with cunning,
Though prideful that he cannot be beat,
The wars of the evil one will come.
His queen rules by his side,
As just and wonderful as he,
She keeps him upright and true,
So that all may love both of them.
He does not stand alone,
Only by the grace of their heavenly lords,
He has seen the gates of heaven,
In holy and prophetic dreams.

Dead Armies

Many do not think it possible,
For the dead to walk the realms,
But there is power,
Dark power,
Capable or raising the dead from their tombs.
In these dark and evil days,
The skeletons and zombies walk,
Destroying the living that walk at night,
Even the innocent, the fragile.
They care not for gold,
Only wanting to see pestilence,
Cover the face of the earth.
Where they go, disease easily follows,
Since these armies do not care,
About anything under the sun.
Debasing living flesh,
To raise new soldiers,
Men, women, children, all,
They kill without thought,
Without mercy.
The living are of no use to them,
All must die and suffer their wrath,
To be raised again in the dusk,
So they can carry on the war.
A dark lord from the north gives them their power,
None can stand before them,
All will fall,
All will fade.

The Mountain Pass

Danger lurks on every peak,
But the mountains must be crossed.
A spine of peaks that stretch,
Across the world and back,
Hiding secrets and realms,
Long forgotten, long lost.
Creatures of evil roam the paths,
Preying on those that they would encounter,
To feed their dark wills,
And weaken frail hearts.
Brave men wander these stretches,
To rid the passes of such filth,
But they always come back,
They always hunt.
Heroes have been lost,
Legends never found,
From the creatures lurking here.
The bravest of souls are the ones,
Who comes here for a simple trek.
To come here unprepared,
Will be a journey most dire,
For if you do not worry yourself,
With what is behind the next cleft,
What waits there may take your soul.

The Drow Princess

In caverns below the earth,
Deep in forgotten realms,
Where the sun never touches the rock,
And light never brings new life.
Cities are kept and breathe,
Life is bustling, but sad.
Mighty warriors, hidden from the light,
With skin black as night,
Hair white as the stars,
But cruel as vipers,
Pitiless as the dragons they keep.
Worshipping dark gods best forgotten,
A princess arises.
Something is different in her,
This dark elf, filled with hope and light,
Breaks free from her royal family,
That oppress all that come under their reign,
To flee to the surface, where again she is in chains.
Crowds want to hang her,
For the crimes of her race,
One man, a human,
Should be opposed to all she is,
But shows her grace, shows her love.
Many despise them for their charity,
She fights to show a new way to her oppressors,
For she was not born evil,
Like so many assume,
But born of goodness amongst the dark.

White Wolf

East of the great mountains,
The great spine of the world,
A creature dwells,
Horrible and ferocious.
Many mistake him for a wolf,
But he is larger, stronger,
Able to rip and tear with little effort.
Woodsmen have hunted him,
To bring his pelt for a bounty,
But he cannot be stopped,
He is the white wolf of Aragband.
Once he was a man,
Noble and arrogant,
Who ruled lands ancient and rich.
Until a gypsy cursed him,
Transformed him to this,
So that he would learn humility,
And be restored to his glory.
Time has forgotten him,
The sun has set on his due,
His humility grew to frustration,
Frustration to anger,
Anger to madness.
He remembers not who he was,
Or what he has to gain,
Just the anger of being forgotten,
Of being hunted by those once his own.

Southern Jungles

Deep to the south of the lands of humans,
Where even the ancient elves refuse to go,
Lay jungles of ancient horrors,
Lying in wait for anyone to enter their home.
These are reptiles, lizards,
That walk like men, but are twice their size.
They even talk and reason,
Build and fashion,
Yet most consider them beasts.
They fear the world outside the jungle,
Outside of the heat they find comfort in.
The gold and jewels they make into weapons,
Realizing not the worth of their crafts,
If they only knew the wealth that lay within their cities,
They would be lords of the world,
Mightier than even the dwarf kings.
But they have been punished,
Exiled,
For what they are,
Nobody thinks them as people.
Their hatred knows no bounds,
For the slaves they have been made into,
At the hands of poachers,
That see them as nothing more than animals.
Fight brave lizardmen,
Fight and prove your worth.
The world needs new warriors,
New blood,
To fight the coming ancient terrors.

Temple Lords

Men-like bulls guard the ancient temples,
Built long ago by forgotten hands.
Even the elves in all their elegance,
Look at wonder at these halls.
The minotaurs do not allow them access,
Secrets within are theirs.
Too many have tried to pry their way in,
But these mighty warriors send them back.
Horrible they are to behold,
Tall and proud with great axes in hand.
These warriors are strong,
Years spent in combat make them equals,
To the greatest warriors of the orc and elven halls.
Yet they are few.
These ancient temples are falling one by one,
As the ancient darkness returns.
These halls to Yahweh are being defiled,
In an attempt to subdue his strength.
The minotaurs fight back this storm,
They will not yield to the night.
Truth is their armour,
Light is their axes,
Yet the night continues to press on.
Many of their number have folded to the infernal,
Many of their brothers have the nobles had to kill.
This civil war will ensue until one is defeated,
Until the darkness overcomes,
Or the light is able to stand firm.

The Paladin

Noble warrior, imbued with the power of Yahweh,
To dispatch the undead and infernal.
He wanders the world,
Fighting for the light,
Fighting for honour,
For an order of knights that may no longer exist.
His morningstar flashes in the night,
As he breaks the oncoming hordes,
To free the innocent,
The meek,
And make them free from tyranny.
He weeps over the state of the world,
He knows a darkness has returned,
To fight it back is his desire,
How this will happen, he does not know.
His duty is simple,
To defend all,
Whether humble or proud,
Even good or evil,
If they are innocent,
He is called to defend.
But he walks the road alone.
No one will join him,
His sanctimonious mission is too much for them.
Greed has no place in his heart,
Nor arrogance.
He fights for righteousness,
Hoping one day, he will find peace in this dark place.

Knights of Sanctity

Riding in file,
In a holy march,
A quest to reclaim the land.
Taken by orcs and demon kin,
The knights ride on.
Gallant horses and mighty men,
Wear armour of polished steel,
Gleaming white in the sunlit hours,
Shining dutifully in the pale moonlight.
Their holy call drives them forth,
Vows of purity not taken lightly,
Ever marching onward to battle,
To purify land and kingdom.
Each anticipates the coming death,
With fearless honour they push forth.
To die is gain,
The eternal peace,
Brought on by promises of the divine.
Sworn to oaths in holy temples,
This order of knights hates all defilers,
Of places of holiness and purity.
The orcs dare not stand against them,
These knights' numbers are too great.
Still the orcs line up for war,
Hoping their ferocity will win out in the end.
These warriors fear not death or pain,
So bravely they charge the fold.
Though the orcish tribes inhabit the fortress,
Captured by nobles of the land,
The knights charge forward,
Lances down,
Shields of faith borne with hope.

Wrath of War

The world is changing,
What was once peaceful and true,
Is now corrupt and debased.
The rumours of war are spreading,
Lenoria is on the brink of destruction,
Too many foes are arising,
Foes of old and ancient terror.
Demons have sprung from the deep,
Balors, fiends of the pit and more.
Guardians of ancient wonder,
Have tried to arise to counter them,
But the lords of heaven have left it,
Left it in the hands of mortals.
The elves, dwarves and humans must unite,
Or else they all will fall.
Too many of these peoples have too much anger,
Too much hatred for ancient grudges,
Uniting will not be an easy task.
Guides are sent,
Knights of holy orders,
To try and correct the old prejudices,
Yet this may not be enough.
The march of the orcs and dead has begun,
Drumbeats are heard on the wind,
To the distant ears of the north and south,
And the east and west.
Fright is filling all peoples' hearts,
Ancient powers may have to come,
To save the children of the heavens,
There is too much to do,
Too much to do before the war comes,
Before the innocent start to perish,
And all that is left,
Is memory.

Purifying Fire

A wizards' wrath descends on the foes,
Scorching flesh and bone,
To weaken their wills,
And blacken their twisted souls.
The fire purifies the stench within,
Removing the taint from this unholiness.
The foes attempt to take the tower,
To claim the power as their own.
The fire continues raining from heaven,
Consuming grass and trees,
So that the great enemy may not advance.
The wizard knows time is short,
His power will not last forever,
So he prays to heaven for reprieve,
To be taken away to serve another day.
Magic has its limit,
When power is not fulfilled.
The fire while doing its mighty work,
Will diminish,
It will fail.
The purifying power will cease,
The corruption will grow again,
A plague inserting itself,
Into the hearts of all around.
Disease it is to feeble minds,
Disrupting created flesh,
To something only the lords of hell can admire.
The fire must continue,
As long as it must, it must continue.
Or all will feel the wrath,
All will fall.

The Ancient River

A mighty river old and pure,
Flows from a single source,
That no one has been able to find.
Many have tried to follow it,
Yet it goes onward,
Onward,
Never to end.
It is rumoured to originate,
In the gardens of Lenoria,
Where the first elves, dwarves and humans were born.
When all people were united under one banner,
Under one truth.
Many have tried to find the garden,
Seeking the river as it cleanses the land.
Its waters are pure and healing,
Seeping with power of the divine.
Many make pilgrimages to these waters,
To heal the plagues and diseases of the flesh,
And the detriments of the soul.
Some see the river itself as divine,
Yet it is no god,
Just has the power of the divine within it.
The elves themselves drew their immortality from it,
The dwarves their keen stonework,
Humans drew their passions.
Other races have tried to corrupt the river,
But it has resisted all attempts.
No dark power has been able to destroy,
The divine power of this river,
A river with no name,
But filled with life.

The Great Sea

Chaotic with storms,
Storms that sink the mightiest galleons,
Ravage the surface of the deep.
The lords of heaven themselves,
Use the sea as a barrier to guard against,
Innocent lands beyond.
Where corruption and greed have yet to reach,
Where orcs and dead have yet to war.
Leviathan and Rahab guard the depths,
Sinking the ships that dare the breadth,
No one has been able to pass,
Without contending with these dragons,
Dragons of the mighty sea.
All races have tried to pass,
Believing there are riches abounding,
On shores of pure sunlight.
Yet no one has seen,
No one has the skill to cross the waves,
That crash on shores and hulls.
The rocks that jut out from suspicious spots,
To ground the ships in the midst of the sea.
Mighty divine power guards the depths,
Where ships and creatures of old find their rest.
Some quest in the sea to hunt the creatures,
Creatures of myth and lore,
To claim a trophy unlike any other.
But the sea will claim them all,
The monsters will emerge and take them down,
Before they can even blink an eye,
Or breathe a cry for help.

Charron's Herald

Some sit in the quiet night,
Before a great battle to come,
Watching the lakes and rivers,
For a herald, a harbinger of doom.
They say when a skiff,
Carrying a single poleman,
Dressed in long robes,
And a skulled head,
Comes up to the shore,
That death has come to them all.
A herald of doom,
Of eternal torment,
To carry souls to the realms of Sheol,
There to be held until the return of majesty.
Some think him a demon,
A servant of dark and angry lords,
But no one knows for sure,
All fear the sight, if and when he comes,
While others pray for hopes that he will not arrive.
If he comes, wars are called off,
Peace is attempted,
So that damnation will not fall.
Everyone fears the boatman,
No one willing to pay his price,
To cross the Styx and see the dead lands,
To see the realms where only some may rest.
Too many fear the pit,
That awaits them in Sheol,
Still others fear the unknown,
That arrives with the Herald of Charron.

Glade of the Druids

Hidden deep in the Elvenwood,
Where trees have long grown,
To hide the realms of natures guardians,
Who prefer to remain hidden,
Secluded.
There is an open glade,
Beautiful it is, filled with heaven's light,
Reaching through the trees,
To streams with shores of flowers,
And cleansing water of starlight.
Ancient wonders are found here,
Buried deep within the soil,
Powers forgotten since long ago.
That the druids quietly protect.
They know the power of the Elvenwood,
Even if the elves who live here do not.
The trees have knowledge unfounded,
Forgotten long ago by all peoples.
The druids fear the evil to come,
That it may reach the glade.
They have prepared for war,
To protect this ancient glade,
So that darkness may not overpower it.
Ancient treemen have answered the call,
Of the ancient archdruid,
To protect what they hold most dear,
The power of nature itself.
This glade is the epicentre of nature's glory,
Some believe to be the Garden of Lenoria itself,
If it is true, the druids are not saying,
But evil is eager to find out,
So that it can set up a throne in the ancient glade.

Nymph Queen

A guardian of the wood and lakes,
This most beautiful creature,
Takes and makes a home.
She is sworn to defend her lands,
Against all perversion of mortal flesh,
With a beauty that enraptures,
Even the strongest of will.
Those that fail to resist her,
Are not able to break the power of her will,
As she commands them as simpletons,
In all aspects of her power.
The realms she lives in,
Is also a home of the elves,
The forest of Symgate,
An alliance to defend it from the outside world.
She is sworn to marry the elven king,
As a symbol of this alliance,
Though they are not able to have offspring,
The marriage is symbolic,
So that all may see the power in their union.
The queen rules her own as her own,
With no influence from others,
Defending the deepest of the woods,
Where ancient powers dwell,
Forgotten, unwanted.
Her allies, apart from the elves, are many,
As she is able to seduce even the strongest man.
Spies all over the world she has put in place,
Making her the most knowledgeable creature alive.
If any would want to know,
The deepest secrets of the world,
They should seek her out.
But beware her beauty,
Or your quest for knowledge will be over,
As you become her most willing slave.

Tower of Night

Deep in the wastes of the east,
Where sand and stone rule the land,
And the dead are present in the long-lasting night.
A tower has been raised,
To signal the rulership of a dark lord,
A lord who neither sleeps nor rests,
But rules with cruelty and malice.
He feasts on the souls of mortals,
Rejoices in the nightmares of children,
And ravages the armies of all.
The orcs and the dead serve him,
They march as one under a banner of doom,
To sound his siren song in the depths,
Of a world that wants to forget him.
Too many have tried to write him off,
As myth, as legend, best left to imagination.
Yet the armies march once more,
The wisemen of the white towers of humans,
And the crystal towers of elves,
Have all foreseen his coming.
Many have ruled from this tower in ages past,
But none have exerted the will of madness,
Madness and malice this lord empowers.
This will sends the armies forward,
With power and cunning unlike any before.
What hope is there that the tower will fall,
With its lord into a pile of rubble?
The stonework is ancient, forgotten by even dwarves,
The workmanship exquisite,
Yet it is evil,
Shall goodness prevail,
When such darkness is present,
In a world that prefers ignorance?

Temptations of Gold

Dwarves hide in their golden halls,
Hoarding the gold they acquire.
Riches so deep and wonderful,
Yet they share it with no one.
They could finance nations and armies,
To be the best they could be,
With gleaming armour,
And razor-sharp swords,
Yet they keep it for themselves,
To make their treasuries vast beyond measure.
Their skills are deep and wonderful,
The most precious monuments,
Of gold and other metals,
Stand tall in their halls.
The yellow shimmer glows in their mountains,
In their kingdoms of stone,
The gold shimmers and shines.
Their hearts are filled with greed,
And the armies of darkness would take it all.
If the dwarves do not seek forgiveness,
For their greed and arrogance,
Then judgment will fall on them.
Their halls are strong and well armed,
Due to the gold their hoard,
But the armies of evil are greater,
Can their gold save them from death?
They cannot take it with them,
There is no place for riches in the death lands,
Yet they try to make themselves wealthier,
Richer in state,
To what end?
What will all these temptations lead to,
If not their utter ruin?

The Guild

Quiet and secretive,
Everyone knows they are there,
But no one knows who is a member.
Like shadows on the walls,
They watch without ceasing,
Biding their time of when to strike,
When to steal,
When to kill.
The fear of their wrath,
Fills the poor and disadvantaged,
As they are the slaves to their will,
The will of the guild's lords.
They take from those that have not,
To make themselves richer,
Though they need not the wealth,
Like all greed they desire more.
Power is also a craving,
Mayors and kings have paid them due,
Giving them work to undue political foes,
To keep their hands clean,
And make themselves seem benevolent,
When indeed they are not.
The guilds have their secrets,
They could tear kingdoms down,
But they do not want a public face,
But to remain hidden, unseen,
Awaiting a time once more,
To steal or kill.

Robed Pilgrim

A mysterious wanderer,
No one knows his name,
Or where he comes from.
Fighting for justice,
Quietly undoing the powers of evil.
Some see him as a prophet,
A return of an ancient priesthood,
A mediator between mortals and heaven.
He does not speak of his mission,
Just visits the lowly places,
Fighting the darkness in the home.
Believing that goodness has to start,
In the heart before the kingdom.
Sure, he believes evil must be fought,
But evil must not take hold,
In the hearts and minds of all people.
He speaks truth and morality,
To all who will listen,
And brings the sword down on those who oppose,
Those who would keep the people,
The innocent, in bondage.
He bears power from heaven,
To accomplish his task.
Many fear his coming,
Knowing they may be a target.
He loathes the darkness,
Persists against it,
Yet shows mercy and justice,
To everyone willing to repent.

Tavern Tales

In every city and town,
The tavern awaits all,
All who would come,
To find work or drink,
Song and dance,
Food and comfort.
Travellers from far and wide,
Find their way to this place,
To speak of their adventures,
To build fame and fortune,
Or to forget the horrors,
Horrors of a coming darkness.
Most are mercenaries,
Swords for hire,
Others are spies, seeking discontent,
In the best place known.
Still others wait for a time,
To rise up and be heroes,
To bring the light of heaven,
In a realm falling to night.
The greatest of heroes are found here,
As they are the brave,
The willing and foolish,
To face any fear,
Any monster,
For those willing to award them coin,
Coin that is much desired for their schemes.
All wait for the right heroes to come,
To find their fill of drink and food,
So that the evils ever present in the world,
Can be fought and subdued.

Forgotten Places

There are places in Lenoria,
Forgotten and alone.
Places of power,
Places of peace,
Where some have seen the passage of time,
And others have slept awaiting their epoch.
In some places elder things await,
Some evil,
Some benevolent,
Yet all await the coming war.
Other places are sullen and forlorn.
No one remembers them,
Though they are important,
To the success of heaven or hell,
But they will be discovered again.
Towers, forests, mountains, valleys,
All have a part to play,
Even if no one is there to guard them.
All will answer the call in the time to come,
The time of the destiny of good or evil.
No one can know what role they will play,
No one can know,
For they have forgotten,
Forgotten the importance of these unknown,
Peaceful and sometimes dark realms.
The war will hinge on the capture,
The conquering of realms of glory.

Bard' s Song

Here comes now the end of the tales,
Of stories old and enemies new,
To those who would listen,
To the songs sung about these times.
Heroes are needed,
Now more than ever.
Armies must soon march,
To fight the darkness,
To combat the slavery to come.
We take for granted,
The freedom we have,
To be heroes everyday,
In the battle for the light.
Songs anew will always be sung,
To warm the hearts of children,
To warm the hearts of warriors,
So that they will rise up and fight,
Since so many want to hide,
Hide away and do nothing.
Cast not your fears away,
For they will give you strength,
To realize what must be fought,
What must be conquered.
Listen to the tales in all the towns,
To learn of what evils to confront,
Get your strength from the cares,
The cares of the people you love.
For they will carry you through,
So that you will have your own song,
Your own song and ballad,
To sing to the next generation.

.

www.ingramcontent.com/pod-product-compliance
Lightning Source LLC
Chambersburg PA
CBHW030714110426
42739CB00029B/387